More praise for Harley Elliott:

"I once included Harley Elliott in a group I referred to as "Poets of the 6th Principle Meridian" (the north-south line used as a base for the Public Land Survey System that laid out the hatch-work of green and brown quadrangles we see as we fly over heartland America). He has lived for many years within a stone's throw of that meridian and his poems often speak as straight as a section-line road about the beating hearts of prairie denizens. The forms of the poems on the pages of Creature Way put me in mind of that characterization; short line lengths make the poems on their pages into graphic depictions of prairie perspectives; apparently simple words put together in what appear to be simple ways are revealed by attentive reading to express insightful truths as intertwined and intense as the tillering subsurface webs that sustain prairie grasses through drought and fire and flood. You owe yourself this conversation with Harley Elliott."

—Roy Beckemeyer, Author of *Mouth Brimming Over* (Blue Cedar Press, 2019)

"Few poets can meditate on a prairie scene (or any scene) with Harley's wicked, intelligent wit. For instance, when climbing through a barbwire fence following a lovely woman, Harley writes, "If she turns and / parts the wires for you / call the preacher." That's all Harley: voice and smarts and humility and romance, all at once."

–Kevin Rabas (Poet Laureate of Kansas, 2017-2019), *All That Jazz*

More praise for Harley Elliott:

"Harley Elliott is a homespun philosopher with a gifted ear and the heart of a laughing scavenger."

    -Steven Hind

"Harley Elliott is the poet who made me want to be a poet. His new book of revelations, *Creature Way,* continues to interrogate the relationship between humans and other living beings--including stones. The poem "Turquoise" asserts, Some say it looks like sky. / Some say it is sky." Artifice collapses. This is an essential book about the cosmos from the poet who changed my life. "

    -Denise Low, Kansas Poet Laureate

Creature Way

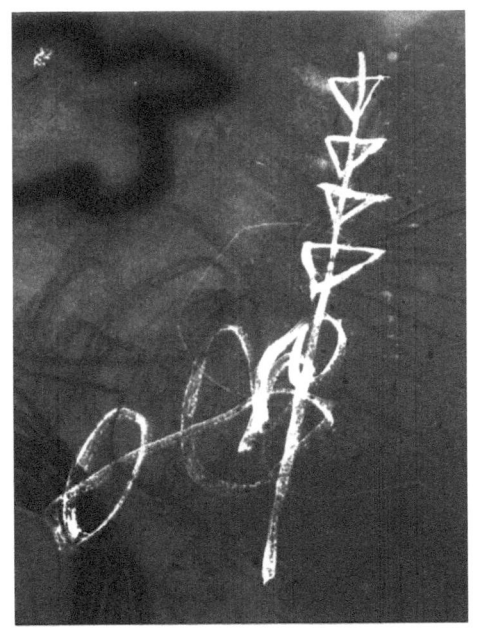

Poems by Harley Elliott

Spartan Press
Kansas City   Missouri

Spartan Press
Kansas City, MO
spartanpresskc.com

Copyright © Harley Elliott, 2020
First Edition: 1 3 5 7 9 10 8 6 4 2
ISBN: 978-1-952411-29-8
LCCN: 2020943568

Cover art: *Bird Songs at Dusk* (detail) by Jane Booth
Author's photo: Ruth Moritz
All rights reserved. No part of this publication may be reproduced or transmitted in any form or by any means, electronic or mechanical, including photocopying, recording or by info retrieval system, without prior written permission from the author.

Acknowledgements:

Many thanks to family and friends for their encouragement and suggestions. Thanks to Lori Brack for always catching me up. Thanks to the editors of the following publications in which some of these poems first appeared:

Hanging Loose, Imagination & Place, Kansas Time + Place, The Mockingheart Review, New Letters, Red Owl, Somewhere Between Kansas City And Denver, Stray Dog

TABLE OF CONTENTS

Getting There / 1

Prairie Courtship / 3

Poetry Conference / 5

Little Hawk / 8

Simple / 9

The Breaking String / 10

Gloria Grahame Invites Me To Lunch / 11

Rainbows For Potatoes / 12

Two Beside The River / 13

Slowly Getting Wiser / 14

Afternoon Window / 16

Loser Werewolf Blues / 17

Still Life 101 / 19

Turquoise / 22

A Friend Goes Out / 23

Prairie Standard Time / 24

Flow / 25

Possum Logic / 27

Two Monks With Problems / 28

The Master Makes A Point / 29

Fragment Of A Head / 31

The Right Dog / 32

Walking In Tall Weeds / 33

Leaders At Play / 35

Medicated / 38

White Gloves / 40

Rules / 42

Boy With Gun / 43

A Political Guide To Unloading Watermelons / 44

The Yodeling Joker / 48

Joyful / 50

Dream Canoe / 51

Time Out / 53

He Wonders / 54

What Modigliani Knew About Skin / 56

Halfway Across The Arkansas River / 57

A Spontaneous Race At The
   Medicine Lodge Peace Treaty Pageant / 58

How To Not Ride A Coyote / 60

What Lawn / 62

Dream Of The Official Pencil / 63

Sleeping By The River / 64

The Sound Of Something Passing / 65

Talking With Birds / 66

Power / 68

Hyena Love / 69

The Most Beautiful Stone In The World / 70

Any Day Now / 73

Hold Tight / 75

Creature Way / 76

First Contact / 78

For
Elaine and Darío
Steven Hind
Bill Sheldon

Getting There

Maybe you had to be there
or more likely wanted to.
It was possibly vital
a goal or destination
that might have had
unerring potential.

Maybe you made elaborate plans
what to take and how much.
You could have just
gone as you were.
You are pretty sure your
arrival would have been
important to somebody.

Maybe trust could have been saved
a fence made true
or a contract signed because
you got there whether
puffing and blowing desperation
or gracefully early.

Maybe you were chosen
an omen set your path.
Maybe you took a desire
seriously getting there
far ahead of yourself.

Maybe there won't turn
out to be like you
think it is. Maybe it
ought to shift for itself
with you right here
breathing down to the
hairs of your body.

Prairie Courtship

When you take her
by the creek road
to hear the owls
and none speak
your next line
should not be
well I guess there are
no owls tonight.

On your stroll across
the prairie it is
unwise to try for a
stolen kiss while she
is examining a rock.

No matter how large
dark and lustrous
her long-lashed eyes
do not use
the word cow.

Before introducing her
to your good old dog
make sure he understands
there is to be no
embracing of legs.

When splaying the
barbwire fence strands
apart so she can
ease through
a gentleman will
refrain from staring
at her bended ass.

If you do and are
transfixed she is
possibly The One
and you probably
don't deserve her.

If she turns and
parts the wires for you
call the preacher.

Poetry Conference

The room was full of
words because the
room was full of poets.
In the tangle of conversation
the very famous poet
was rolling a joint and
discussing Michelangelo's ass.
The quiet poet with
breasts smiled and
said no fifty times.
The really drunk poet
sustained fifty refusals
after he'd begged her to
please let him kiss it.
The poet who never got
around to writing anything
down was explaining
his theory of everything.
The noted academic
poet had a sort
of smile and radiated
charming wisdom.
The incredibly drunk poet
swore twenty times he'd
leave her in peace if
she'd only let him touch it
and was told it wouldn't
happen twenty times.

The poet of self love
assessed the assembled
vulnerabilities for
a late night approach.
The very famous poet
passed the smoke and
began speaking in hums.
The noted academic poet
thought: drugs cops scandal
should be home in
bed with his wife.
Wait. Where was his wife?
Over all the shouted
names of poems and poets
in the undertow of
babble about language
the poet with breasts
denied for the tenth
time the hopelessly drunk
poet who had sobbed ten
times the world would
be in order if she'd
just let him see it.
The very famous
poet felt more famous.
The poet who kept
it to herself thought
she might write a poem.
The nervous academic
prepared his statement.

The terminally drunk poet
fell unconscious and
dreamt about it.
The not sure he was
a poet yet in the
corner kept his
cakehole shut.

Little Hawk

There was a man once
called Swoop Of A Bird.
I am not the only one
who has flown to your

dance with air
urgent song lifting those
lowdown roadside clouds.
The eye that sees

weeps a dark comma
and swiftly goes.
You have been sweeter
than I deserved.

Simple

No one really knows
how many words the
Inuit have for snow
since it has not
yet stopped snowing.

Corn is our mother
now toyed with
and violated. A false
mother has been made
in her place.

The measurements
called Time are
a convenient fairytale.
Stones live so
slowly one breath
spans generations.

Seated at a rushing
riverside the girl's
hands dart and pounce
above the water
playing a piano that
lives in her fingertips.

Some snows
are anonymous
content in their being.

The Breaking String

Factor x lies heavy
in the whisper of the string.
The guitar is going to lose a muscle . . .

understanding races
the event to the brain
  a twinge of sparrow
  oblivious to 22 caliber
  high velocity suddenly there

the guitar string murmurs
the bridge drops a cable
air parts the tight rope
the swinging vine
the axis shudders
continents snap.

Now at the edges
of the hole in the song
let the playing hand gather

weave over discord in a moment
weave over sorrow
weave over loss.

Gloria Grahame Invites Me To Lunch

only 10 years conscious glutting popcorn
and Gloria Grahame smirks
a red smear of lips
into my life astride
the neck of an elephant

shining arms and
legs call out with
the urgency of candy
hands on hips and
hips rocking a mystery
of sequins back and forth

slitted eyes promising the
greatest show on earth
like tomorrows fried
chicken but better

congeals my popcorn
chills the hairlets of my neck
undulating up a strange
sweaty hunger centered on that
for which I did not have a name

and when the inevitable
lights come up Gloria
goes on to portray
many slutty dames and
I to discover it
really wasn't about food

Rainbows For Potatoes

Ah yes the birds the
chorus of leaders warbled
the flowers even the
insistent green of
grass and trees all
quite beautiful not
to mention the
kittens and puppies.

Three cheers for the
sweetness and the light.
Cue the cellos!
Release the bluebirds!

We did not respond.
We had requested bread
but received trinkets.
We asked for potatoes and
they gave us rainbows.
Dyed-blue sparrows flapped
twice and nose-dived
into the feverish dust.

Starving on slogans
we had hoped for reason.
Now the remedy is clear.
Our skeletons rise.
A signal is given.

Two Beside The River

Two walk bone light
beside the river

conflict and comfort
wounds of memory

keep step with
the rivers sweep

for those who no longer
breathe this flow

they draw it in
there is no where

it comes from
where it goes

each knowing the other
beyond breath and one

step after another
beside this river.

Slowly Getting Wiser

In adolescence you idolized
far above your station
a girl whose charms made
the air around her tremble
and she dropped the hammer
on your little cupcake

and worse she did this
by simply not knowing
you existed.
You were learning.

Time came when
you expected nothing
and nothing was received
no bowls of dates
no candied pears
no yon dusky beauties.

Perfect.

Now you settle between
the poles of desire and dismay
in shadows upon shadows
the old horse of a refrigerator
shudders and snorts.

Finally you think you
begin to get a clue.

Should you contact who
might be the love of your
life and announce you are
ready for your interview?
No. Not yet.

Afternoon Window

The branch knows the grasp
of the resting hawks talons

a brief alliance like
the space between breeze

and billowing curtain
or these finger

tips caressing fine skin
these blossoming clouds

drifting a heartbeat
ahead of their shadows.

Loser Werewolf Blues

Even as a whelp
lurking on midnights
edge it was always
your innocence to be
pissing in all
the wrong flowerbeds.
Lights! Sirens! Hounds!
A wet pant leg
on the getaway.

There were days of
dancing happy moonlight
reveling in your
hairy self and
howling for the
pure nonsense of it
but from the beginning
you never understood
the concept of menace.

And now they're tracking
your spoor and some
savvy vigilante proclaims
From the look a
this turd I'd say
it's a werewolf.
And a big one.

That would be you
who roamed the
night without bloodlust.
Who could have been
a wrestling star if
you'd only bulked up.
You who tried to
shave your forehead.

You never got it right
you sorry example
of lupine ambition
and so the real
werewolves say
you'll have to go.

Still Life 101

1.
Parables don't just rise from
golden light in the pale
bright woods where we
rest overcoated bodies in
a drift of leaves

or the congress of grackles
shifting discussion from tree
to tree maybe about two
humans who have done the
incredible by not moving.

It is all parable
as Teacher discovers when he
stands too fast and sways
anchoring himself to his
overcoat pockets while
the birds leap a brief
corona on the trees

and dive into the wind. Teacher
returning to himself observes
the Great Spirit has spoken.

2.
Smoke from long gone lodges
still tangles in this dirt.
Our time to sit here now
forearms on knees above
the crawl of muddy river

which has been given a name
as has the land we cover
and the larger land it
supposes itself within.

Being is outside that grid
like the small bird Teacher
points his chin at
flitting in and away
scouting different angles

a small fast dance
on the borders of identity
so it will be always
radiating from this
the simplest moment

dirt
river
little brown bird.

3.
Bellycrawling the half mile
of dry grass gully
the hundreds of feeding geese
we are supposed to see
when peering over the edge

are somewhere else and have
left thousands of purple
and white goose turds
which Teacher advises can
only be watched so long.

We fall back to the sky
a blue that with a growing
rush two geese cross over.
Above the rowing of wings
one turns to the other

honks a syllable

the Teacher making confident
observation of two humans
skygazing unarmed unambitious
behavior worth noting
in that one wise squank

and then all flown and
still flying now
the breath of that moment
in this great sweep of wind.

Turquoise

Hard to be false
with turquoise while
turquoise never lies.

Some say it looks like sky.
Some say it is sky.
An eye brought by rain
opens in the earth.

Hard to be false
to that bright glance
since turquoise
is so true.

A Friend Goes Out

He shot himself.
The diagnosis was
dementia the promise
a dissolving mind.

He could not say
what world his brain
wandered him into
each new moment
shuffling together
the cards of his memory.
It was a game
he could not play.
If he thought of
his friends and lovers
once he'd decided
he must have been
certain he was

favoring us
with his absence
bequeathing only the
best versions of himself
as a friend when
leaving would do.

Prairie Standard Time

Here comes a cloud
and there it goes
dissolved in quick time.

Here lies a stone
bedded in the
dirt of centuries
giving itself up
molecule by molecule
in the slow
stretch of time.

Here coyote cricket
bluestem lark indigo
all that thrive and pass
know themselves by
other names in journey
through their times.

Here a footprint
alone and off the clock.
You are free
horizon to horizon
to choose the time
for your life.

Flow

Hovering in starlight on the
lush bank of wide
rapid black water
scribbles of white leaping
language of where the
big rocks lay
powerful in its
relentless going like
the childhood eternity
I used to imagine
knowing I would sleep
before it ended.

Behind me in the dark
a granddaughter learns
to tap dance. The clatter
of metal-capped steps
echoes the horseshoes
on the mare her sister rode
one day before and a
river dancing nightly.

Soon I will leave this flow
and ride a train
stopped west of Chicago
because the intercom
informs us the train has
struck a trespasser and

explaining there will be
some delay adds
Thank you for riding Amtrak.

Down the line the conductor
will watch smokers fogging
up Iowa and say he's
from L.A. and five or six
people jump in front of
trains there every week.
He will say we lost three hours
and won't know why the
guy couldn't have chosen
one of the freight trains
hell they run
through there all the time.

But now only deep river
rushing a music of
water and darkness.
I could stand
here three hours
years a simple
bobble on the journey.
Later I will know
more civilized forces
and someone else will
choose to dive.
Tonight for all our sakes
the river carries on.
The dancers will dance the
horses will run
like water forever.

Possum Logic

In the car light
possum shambles
cringes
and smiling makes a break

Certain things we have
come to depend on
insistence on habit
or deficiency of neurons
your curse of a comic death
on every given road

In car light we think
ugly stupid ugly and stupid
not enough hair to make a hide
your hopeless feint and shuffle

cancel each other out
this sleep you do
not walk away from
no stinking dignity
the light

the world
turned inside out
for reasons of your own
no tricks no kicks
just where it's at

Two Monks With Problems

What seems to be your problem?
I don't have a problem.
That is a problem.
Ah I see.
There's another.
Ah I'm sorry.
Please. You are making too many problems.
I am only trying to be normal.
Stop. Let us say we are dreaming.

The Master Makes A Point

X and Y visit a
farm of friends in
the swelter of July.
X in sneakers and
heat-sagged jeans
digs in the garden
streaming sweat.

Y lolls in a lawn chair
mirror sunglasses
and cutoffs
beer in one hand
smoke in the other
a sip here a drag there
breaking little sweat.

Damn thinks X
It's hot here I am
helping out and Y
thinks he's at the beach.
With every shovel thrust
X feels more superior.

Heading for the farmhouse
to rehydrate he
passes in front of Y
sweaty back bowed

shovel dragging as if
it too has been
depleted by the
nobility of labor.

X drinks cool water
glances out the window
at Y still in repose
thinks damn Y
ain't doin' shit.
Returning to his labors
X drags past again
shovel bumping listlessly
behind,   Every cell sighs
righteous weariness.

Y examines the dramatic
exhaustion shambling by
notes the swollen
ego resentment and
sticks a pin in it
with his best fake
baronial Texan drawl:

When you get done
there Gomez you can
dig me a swimming pool.

Fragment Of A Head

Yellow jasper a stone
that chips like glass
somehow abraded
and polished to
a shining finish.

Her chin her lips
how the tender flesh
curves into both
sorrow and joy.

Above her chin her lips
only smooth scalloped
fractures and space
but what is there says all.

What hands called
out such truth
and what hands
struck it down?

To have so deeply
fused hope and regret
some among those
drillers grinders sanders
must have believed in her
as I believe in her
her chin her lips
my joy my sorrow.

The Right Dog

To greet peacekeepers
as equals and scout
out approaching evil
give us a dog with
a good nose for intentions

one with plenty of
genetic tangle in
its history and enough
wolf spark to carry
itself as if it belonged
to the world at large.

Let us have a dog who
waits for the right signal
but knows how to play
and when sitting side by
side this dog leans
on you just a little
to let you know.

Walking In Tall Weeds

You part the weeds
these thick plants swept
into one rank category
useless or contrary to
the agricultural plan.

Ticks disengage at your
passing warmth and drop on
to a long crawl for blood.
Mosquitos tune you in.
Still you part the weeds.

Chiggers make you
wish your crotch belonged
to someone else.
You must be crazy
but you part the weeds
brushed aside
and closing behind.

Some twitch your cuffs
and sign your arms with
tiny marks as swimming
on your feet through
heavy green breath
you part the weeds.

Destination is memory
and time only footsteps
walking in tall weeds.
You reach out.

Leaders At Play

It was the biggest game in town.
The ante alone was
evidence of hazardous leakage.
Pile of glowing waste
by pile of glowing waste
landed in the pot
and the cards went out.

There was a slitting of eyes
and slotting of mouths.
First bets were cautious
leading with a spotted owl.

I'll see your endangered species
and raise you a selective famine.
Cover that famine and I'll
raise an oceanic garbage island.

The kitty grew. Some dropped
out early having only
stakes of a few million
starving infants and
scatters of exotic plagues
until only two remained.

I'll see your polluted aquifer
and raise you one million
units of cannon fodder.

Got that covered and I'll
add a severed rain forest.
Very well. My ravaged forest
and raise a couple
of over-heated oceans.
No problem.

And so while beings
frolicked elsewhere they
discarded and drew into
a duel of sweaty mayhem
and catastrophe the two
leaders calling and raising
until they were both all in.

I got you with a
mighty flush of spades.
Hold on. Full house
despots over knaves.
Sonofabitch.

When the winning leader
cashed out it took
the tallyman all night
to catalog the pot
and the planetary fate
fell just short
of a dead cinder.

It would cost the losers
many pennies to clean
things up and the
winner stood to clean up
big time on the deal as well
or so the story goes.

Medicated

When you're home alone
and all fucked up
there are no questions
only answers.

Of course let us
lie down here with the
lion and the lamb
since we're all in
this together and
anything is possible.

You could go out
to the curb and wave
your junk like a flag.
Everyone would understand
and the answer
to what could be
simpler is nothing.

You take your meds
and existence breaks
down to the framework
when men first made
Eve the patsy.

Oh there are dues
to be paid your
bathrobe flaps and
your slippers agree.
Clearly the one hundred
percent solution
is global love.

Politics and all the
silly isms will be
sorted out once
we scrape the
scales from our eyes.
Yes we can work this out.

But love must start somewhere
and you appoint yourself
the prime mover.
You make a note
to smile at the mailman.
World Peace. No lie.
But then suddenly
It's time for bed.

White Gloves

The snow fell in the night.
On the television
the strangler kissed
his snow white gloves

they pulsed like a throat
in love with his hands.

Snow White was
waiting in the forest
autumn rain raising
a mist on white gloves.

The composer who was
responsible for sound effects
couldn't sleep.
On the piano
white gloves sighed

a lingering dream of concertos
at their fingertips.

The snow fell in the night.
In the head of the man
who watched the television
a history of the earth

began to unroll
where comics and killers
put on white gloves
and went out in the night.

The snow falls on the head
of a man in white gloves.
His covered hands shine
where he walks
between laughter and death.

Rules

Back and forth
across the street
through the early
morning fog
two male redbirds
chase each other.

It seems to be
about rules and
who gets to
make them and
who dares to
break them.

We could name them
nation A and nation B
yes and no
you and me
these two red
darts back and
forth in the
heavy pearled air

as advantage is
lost or expanded
blind to the
flaw the possibility
the wisdom of living
on the cusp.

Boy With Gun

First a sparrow and a
small coppery sphere.
Sometimes momentary shame
loses to the power
to make things fall.

He grows in the romance
of velocity and range
this boy a question
and this gun the answer.

We know nothing
of who or what
he may target
or in the name
of who or what.

We do know he
believes he knows
a truth he
will soon reveal

this boy with
no more questions
and this gun
with all the answers.

A Political Guide To Unloading Watermelons

The open top split semi load of watermelons
bedded in tiers of prairie hay arrives
to be unloaded hand to hand by a line
of men none of whom want to be

THE DIGGER at the head of the line
chosen by the foreman to paw melons
out of sour dusty scratchy hay
wades into the truck with a certain
sweaty rectitude since the assignment
proves he is the least willing
to kiss ass and knocks swatches
of old hay off the front top row
while others live with their ass
kissing abilities in order to be

THE PASSERS who will toss
melons to each other
carefully if the fat dark
green Texas Black Diamonds
which always include
bicep busting monsters
more freely if the smaller oval
dark striped Irish Greys
all of them wondering at
some time in the process
who names these things

while the line expands deeper
into the truck except for
the end man who dumps
each melon in the scale pan to
have weight scrawled on
in thick black crayon by

THE MARKER who is either the
oldest or shortest or best
ass kisser of the crew who only
has to mark and lift each
melon from scale to cart
but inherits the ritual of
calling out each weight
and whatever wit he can
40! 32! 61! HERNIA!
until the cart fills and

THE CARTERS return with one
they just emptied tiering
melons three high and
twenty wide chocked with
two by fours exchanging empty
for full and watching how
fast the empty cart loads
so they can dawdle and
claim concern for proper
alignment if yelled at
while back on the line

THE MELON that will have
an accident comes halfway
through the load as one
passer signals another and
said melon is fumbled
between them to the floor
with only enough force to
cause a gentle split
over which everyone
mimes regret and the
melon goes to the cooler
as unloading resumes smoother
now that a melon is chilling
laughing through sweat
and dust and the
calls of the marker
31! 27! 59! BIG MAMA!
finishing as they are
supposed to in under
two hours because

THE BOSS can see them
out his office window
as they leave the truck
shaking dust and hay
the boss makes a
mental note not to
go out to the warehouse
for fifteen minutes
which he knows is

slightly longer than it
will take the crew
joking and lounging
on green net bags of
squeaking cabbages in
the cooler to devour
their sacrificial melon
sliced and served
fairly by

THE FOREMAN who
nevertheless still expects
to get his ass kissed
since he expects to
be kissing the boss's ass
before the day is over
but sees the crew
is too melon
satisfied to kiss
ass now but it's
not five o'clock yet
so he wisely smiles
and wipes his
hands and says
it's time to
go to work.

The Yodeling Joker

He gangbustered into town
and all the stoplights died.
Just to show he was serious
he licked the color
out of the sunset
and tied a knot in the wind
or said he did.
The powerhouse took note

but they were yodeled
into a headlock trance
and soon were voting
for a chimpanzee
in every tree and a
typewriter for every
chimpanzee as well
as inventing fish jello
and garlic cola to sell
to the culturally insecure.

The Republic pulled the
covers over its head
and all the preachers
quickly learned to yodel.
Politicians stayed
home and masturbated.
Cash registers broke

down in tears.
Violins gave up the ghost.
We forgot how to make bread.

He has us in
a kind of thrall the
powers excused themselves
and sold us a lurch
to be left in
and wisdom remained
in no danger
of being discovered.

Joyful

A lake above a lake.
Between them the

dancer shouts praise
and kicks one leg.

Birds startle
from both waters.

Dream Canoe

The sky is hot and
the furrows deep in
this fresh plowed field
extending in all directions
to a blurry horizon.

You are at the back
end of the canoe
carrying it by the crossbar
stumbling over clods
canoe banging the side
of your knee each step

and carrying the front
bald crown and hanging
bookbag is Allen Ginsberg.

You have no sense of
where you are going or why
a canoe is needed there.

The only destination in sight
is more plowed field
but it seems important
that you continue.

A sound comes loud behind.
You both stop lower
the canoe and watch
a helicopter pass over
grow slowly smaller ahead
lost in the sky.

Allen Ginsberg and you have
not spoken to each other.
The two of you bend
pick up the canoe
set your grip
carry on.

Time Out

I caress the midnight
 roses and am caressed back.
Undulating waves of
deep blood petals
lap my fingers.

Settling on the hairs
of my forearm
a little bristle-humped
mechanical dragon
fiercely selects probes
and drinks itself red.

Under stars shapes
shift dark on dark
becoming black cattle.
That drone in the night
is the mind of the herd.

This might be where
I'm supposed to ask
what's it all about
and who am I
anyway but there is
clearly no time in
these moments for
nonsense like that.

He Wonders

He wonders if he remembered
to wash his feet
the nights his children
were conceived.
He thought it would
certainly be best
if he had.

He wonders where all
the people who pass
by are going
and what the hell
the hurry is.

He wonders what happened
to morning frost
the distant jangle
of flying geese
the breakfast the lunch
the supper the sleep.

He's been told to stop
scrabbling his fingers
but once a day
he hitches the team
strap by strap
buckle by buckle

because he likes
the steam of the horses
and his own breath.

He thinks his hands
are strangers now
and wonders why
his gaze always
ends on his knees

reminds himself to
face the river
of light on linoleum
the flow of footsteps
the receding hallway.

What Modigliani Knew About Skin

Officially titled reclining or pink
her photograph has been taken and
widely passed around.
Nothing has changed: her hips
still enclose the world
her eyes still define it

stretching away in her
late afternoon repose
saying   you tell me baby.

Halfway Across The Arkansas River

One stands waist deep
in the water.
Another calls from the
far bank to ask
how he feels.

The one looks
into the water rushing
past his belt
his wavering jeans
and blue tennis shoes
anchored in gravel.

His own face
peers up at him
water dark and twitching
to break free for
the Gulf of Mexico.

One face nods
to the other face
exactly who and
where he is.
He calls back.

I feel like an old man
up to his ass
in the middle
of a cold river.

A Spontanous Race At The Medicine Lodge Peace Treaty Pageant

One of the runners they think
is Northern Cheyenne or
maybe Arapaho hard to tell
from the dark middle of the
football field and they'd
already turned the far
curve of the track before
the drumming of their feet
swerved everyones eye.
The other runner they are
pretty sure is Arapaho
but maybe not.

They run full bore in
and out of the pole light pools
one wearing red and yellow
feather discs he fancydanced
in earlier   the other
jeans T-shirt and ball cap
equal in stride though
no one sees a stride
just four knees pumping
four elbows two chins
upraised side by side.

Now encouragements are called
since they know they
are seeing a race and
they are sure one of the
racers is Northern Cheyenne
but the darkness the speed

and who cares   the race has
become its own creature
raises every voice in praise
of the symmetry of their
effort calling out to the
heart of the running.

Down the stretch they
shook the ground together.
The fancydancer lost no feathers.
Might-Be-Arapaho kept
his baseball cap.
They all forgot who won.

How To Not Ride A Coyote

choose any coyote
saddle it with mystery
and ride off beside the point

the coyote will
return without you

old ones remember when
it was not a lost art
they say in those days
not riding a coyote was
an honorable pursuit

if we insist it is a trickster
that is the first trick
yodeling on the periphery
of labels and words
it has played on us

just when you think you've
got it right astride a
coyote on a cliff at sunset
it slips away
when the movie of your life
comes out you're riding
an idea of a coyote

I was out one day
not riding a coyote
a pleasurable experience
enhancing every encounter
I made good time since
a coyote I was not riding was
not waiting for me at each door

if you think you see other
people riding coyotes
leave town

What Lawn

at the age of sixty I who
always scorned such
property wet dreams
attempt to grow a lawn

time now embraced with
geometry and schedule
the dispensing of morning water
evening water
morning water
evening water
to skinny exclamations of grass

a credible plant muse travels
far to plant encouraging
violets by my door
neighbors smile more to
signal my correctness

but I will mind the snare
of a thing representing
my core
even if it thrives so well
that people say nice lawn
I'll remember to say what lawn

Dream Of The Official Pencil

Deskside with El Presidente
he presents me with
a black pencil
which slowly turns white.

Did I mention I would
piss on the President
if he was on fire
but probably at
the last moment.

But the jury will disregard
that last statement.
We are all about that pencil.

A poet is awarded
a pencil by the Leader
and it has the trick
of becoming its opposite
and white in the bargain.

With such dangerous
ambiguity what can
poets do but awaken
despair the Commander
and check all their
pencils for trueness.

Sleeping By The River

Alone with dark
the skull of the field mouse
might suddenly say
Fast Runner was my kin

and fade back slowly into bone.
Words fly away in the
static of cottonwoods.

Shoulderblades to dirt
things made by hand have been shaping
your life like that Chinese puzzle of
coathangers you wrestled one day.
These knock on the
edge of your dreams.
You sign treaties all night.

Between your nose and the stars
one long breath goes by:
that secret roar
we call the wind.

The Sound Of Something Passing

A man hears it one morning
on his way to be shot.

The ledge jumper
hears it just before.

Somebodys relative has it
tumbling in their ear all day.

A locomotive in the blizzard.
A wing against our heads.

Talking With Birds

The journey is difficult.
The sojourner needs
an encouraging song.

You are checking your maps
in a stutter of wind when
robins land with a
flounce and right away
begin to testify.

Red blue and black
known for their simplicity
have little to say
the eternal question softly
loaded in each wing.

At a choice of crossroads
larks and doves conjure
courtship and loss
to guide your path.

You call out salutes
for the gaze of hawks
and sweet nothings
to countless little
brown birds cleverly
disguised as each other.

You walk on even though
it's all a dream caught
in the rush of stars.
Somewhere along the way
you think you get
the raven's joke.

Power

Words slowly wounded
finally scream
they will signify
whatever is required.

Crows call alarm
and leave the premises.
They know by heart
the desires men carry.

A man's voice is taken.
A woman falls and
the earth trembles.
Children look up into
the eyes of their fate.

Hyena Love

There we were
cavorting like hyenas
in a snowstorm
biting the air
with our wicked smiles
nipping and tumbling
and slobbering up
the landscape.

Yes hyena love
is reeking hot
as volcanic breath
a frenzy of laughter
and ridiculous passion.

They say there is
nothing sadder than
a hyena with a
broken heart but
we know better
don't we wild howler?

Leaping time and space
the same moon
informs us we will
always be each others
beautiful laughing scavenger.

The Most Beautiful Stone In The World

was tide carried onto
sand near Huanchaco, Peru
a moment of oceanic
give and take that
intersected with the path
of a man who recognized
the most beautiful
stone in the world.

Water smooth swirls
red purple green blue
a portable nebula wet
in the palm of his hand.
For that moment he
called it his.

Then the murmuring ocean
and sky reminded him
of arrogance of ownership
and illusion of attachment
so the stone became a test
in which he was invited
to resist himself.
To remain true he
threw it back to the sea
continuing along the shore
sadness at loss shifting
to pleasure at gain.

Even the Buddha might
approve that he was now
the man who had refused
to be burdened by
the most beautiful stone
in the world.

Then before his feet
a wave withdrew and
left behind the
same beautiful stone.
Amazed he plucked up
his reward for demonstrating
freedom from desire.

But wait he said to the
nothingness at large
this is surely a
double test of my
claimed convictions
and so he cast it
once again into the
rolling sea vowing
if it returned it would
live in his pocket.

This time the cosmos
believed him.
Somewhere in the
vast Pacific waters

still lives the most
beautiful stone in the world
and the hand that
holds the memory
carries on.

Any Day Now

Like this one where
the dawn was not rosy
the sky is no one's
favorite blue and the
check is not in the mail

and here you are again
telling us what's what
with your drunken uncle
smile like you've just been
face-humped by an angel.
Blissful assurance!
Radiant certainty!
and all in the teeth of
your approaching shadow.

Beg pardon but don't
talk to me as if
you know or even
as if I know
the first or last
thing of any thing.
In the wingbeat of that
shadow we might
well lose ourselves

to every nuance
stir of dust up to twigs
yearning in swollen
unison to come green

enough to let us know
even and especially on
this sob story of a day
we should now stop talking.

Hold Tight

My friend in life
you were the spark
and I was the ember.

My friend in passing
the wings fall silent.

My friend in death
our words still reach
our dreams still touch.
Hold tight.

Creature Way

So often comes a
battle of loud egos
and cities rotting
from the top down.

The Big Thumb hovers
at the curve of your head.
Treachery and corruption
are honeymooning
just around the corner.

And there you are
Young Striver
poised to discover an
honorable path through
this tangle of power.

Once you could simply
follow your dog
and trust your horse
but the animals
are now all busy
saving themselves.

Gather up their phantoms
the memory shadow
of glancing wolves

ghostly drum of
mustangs running true.

They call out to you.
To lose the human
stain you will
become a creature
and so create the
nature of your way.

First Contact

I am reaching out
in that sudden
fragile shift between
a whisper and a tickle

from the quiet dance
of my breath
beyond words or reason
I am reaching out

past the point
of no regret to
answer a radiating
bloom of invitation

here we are
my hand is a wing
your skin the sky

Harley Elliott lives and writes in Salina, Kansas. He has published eleven books of poetry, a children's book and a non-fiction memoir. He intends his work to fall in the cracks between categories.

This project was made possible, in part, by generous support from the Osage Arts Community.

Osage Arts Community provides temporary time, space and support for the creation of new artistic works in a retreat format, serving creative people of all kinds — visual artists, composers, poets, fiction and nonfiction writers. Located on a 152-acre farm in an isolated rural mountainside setting in Central Missouri and bordered by ¾ of a mile of the Gasconade River, OAC provides residencies to those working alone, as well as welcoming collaborative teams, offering living space and workspace in a country environment to emerging and mid-career artists. For more information, visit us at www.osageac.org

Osage Arts Community

www.ingramcontent.com/pod-product-compliance
Lightning Source LLC
Chambersburg PA
CBHW030345100526
44592CB00010B/833